GW00778070

30130 089696719

Permission to Cry

A play

David Campton

Samuel French—London
New York-Toronto-Hollywood

CHARACTERS

Julia Gibbon, MP
Councillor Eldon-Pugh
Susan Little
Penelope Wright ("Pen")
Dr Semple, MP

The parts of Councillor Eldon-Pugh and Dr Semple can
be played as either male or female

The setting is a bare stage

Time — the present

AUTHOR'S NOTE

Throughout a large part of the play characters are thinking one thing while saying something entirely different. For instance in her first scene with Susan, alarm bells begin to ring for Julia at the first mention of a rally but she continues to chat on a superficial level; and in her scene with Pen, the reason for her visit is if possible to dissuade Pen from attending the rally. Always be aware of the thought behind the words.

The flashbacks all take place in Julia's mind — which is why only she hears the crowd in her scene with Pen (the accident has in fact already happened).

The sound effects are important if only to signal to the audience the switch into Julia's thoughts.

*Other plays by David Campton
published by Samuel French Ltd:*

After Midnight — Before Dawn
Cagebirds
Can You Hear the Music?
Cards, Cups and Crystal Ball
Do-It-Yourself Frankenstein Outfit
Evergreens
Everybody's Friend
Life and Death of Almost Everybody
Mixed Doubles (with others)
Mrs Meadowsweet
Now and Then
Our Branch in Brussels
Parcel
Relics
Singing in the Wilderness
Smile
Us and Them
What Are You Doing Here?
Who Calls?
Winter of 1917
Zodiac

PERMISSION TO CRY

A bare stage, with a solitary chair to one side

Julia and Councillor Eldon-Pugh enter to a patter of applause

Julia sits, smiling a fixed, artificial smile. Councillor Eldon-Pugh advances C *and addresses the audience*

Clr Eldon-Pugh Ladies — and gentlemen, of course — our speaker needs no introduction from me.

Julia (*still smiling rigidly*) Which won't stop you from introducing her at length.

Clr Eldon-Pugh As you are well aware, Julia Gibbon MP is one of our rising politicians, whose elevation in the last cabinet reshuffle to the position of Junior Minister at the Home Office was warmly welcomed by one and all. I do not propose to go on and on, but I believe we are entitled to a little self-congratulation on our double coup for, not only do we have her with us tonight ... (*he searches through his notes*) but ... I don't need to remind anyone of our annual fête, at which we raised the record sum of ... about ... (*he gives up the search*). I'm sure our Treasurer has the exact figure, which I can assure you is impressive. A fête opened by none other than tonight's speaker. A memorable day, if I may say so, and I hope it was as memorable for her as it was for all of us.

Julia If only I could forget it ...

There is the sound of a garden party, with a small crowd and distant band

(*Standing*) If only … If only … If only …

Councillor Eldon-Pugh swoops on her, takes her arm and steers her around the crowds

Clr Eldon-Pugh Well, we can say that our fête has been well and truly opened. An inspirational address. Exactly what our supporters were waiting to hear. I believe you said something like it on *Any Questions*, but of course this was longer and in the flesh. So much more inspiring to hear the words in the flesh I always say. I believe you met our Treasurer earlier. With his lady wife. A very reliable person. Rock solid. And we all need reassurance, don't we? Especially these days when black seems to turn into white overnight in a manner of speaking. I … Ah this is — er … our oldest supporter. Do you think a photograph with our oldest? Shaking hands, maybe? The *Echo* photographer is around somewhere. Probably in the refreshment tent. Can you wheel the chair to the refreshment tent, dear? That's nice … Now what was I saying? We need people at the top who can be relied on.

Susan enters and hovers at a respectful distance

Susan Oh, Miss Gibbon …
Clr Eldon-Pugh Ah, this is … er … from the *Echo*. A small newspaper by Fleet Street standards, but a sturdily independent voice on local matters. I expect we shall be reported on the front page. Would you … ?
Julia Go ahead.
Susan Do I call you Minister?
Julia Call me what you like as long as you report what I say, and not what you think I ought to have said.
Susan The editor asked me to get a few personal details.
Clr Eldon-Pugh Our supporters like personal details.
Julia How — personal?
Susan Oh, not that sort of personal. I mean …
Clr Eldon-Pugh I'm sure our supporters have no interest in

personal details of *that* sort — whatever they may be. After all, the *Echo* is not the *News of the World*. Not that the Minister would have any such ... I mean ... I'll meet you at the refreshment tent in a moment, shall I?

Councillor Eldon-Pugh exits

Julia You haven't been doing this job very long, have you?

Susan Does it show so awfully?

Julia Aren't you really angling for a Women's Page exclusive? "Julia Gibbon occupies her spare time knitting bedsocks."

Susan Gosh. Do you?

Julia Never enough spare time. This is a twenty-five-hour day job, eight days a week.

Susan Miss — er — Minister — after what you were saying just now about law and order ——

Julia I hope you got that down accurately.

Susan We had a copy of the speech. I was just wondering if you had any comment on this afternoon's disturbances.

Julia I didn't observe any trouble around the refreshment tent.

Susan There was a news flash on the radio while you were talking.

Julia And I hoped I was holding the audience spellbound.

Susan Our photographer was listening to the cricket. It seems there was a rally in London.

Julia Fast overtaking cricket as a national pastime. I expect the police had it under control.

Susan According to the radio there was some trouble with the horses.

Julia I understood it was to be an unauthorized march, not a point-to-point.

Susan There were several casualties.

Julia Oh. I'm sorry.

Susan One person died.

Julia Really? You have my assurance the incident will be fully investigated. You can quote me ... The Chairperson seems to be having some difficulty with the oldest supporter.

Susan There weren't many details. After the flash the radio went back to cricket.

Julia Very British. Perhaps you'd better not quote that.

Susan But — having the same job — well, sort of — made it more personal like for me.

Julia Job?

Susan She was a journalist.

Julia She?

Susan You could almost say she died in the line of duty.

Julia Do they … ? Did the radio … ? Was there a name?

Susan Something like … was it — Wright? That's it. Penny Wright. I remembering thinking, "funny name for a journalist". I mean — well — like a baker named Bun. I think I'd heard of her. At least she'll be headline news for a while. If that's any consolation.

Julia (*dully*) No.

Susan No, I don't suppose it is really. You did say there'll be an enquiry, didn't you?

Julia (*in a shocked whisper*) No.

Susan I thought … In your speech you said we should back the forces of law and order.

Julia (*far away*) Why?

Susan Our editor is very strong on law and order. Especially on the new estates.

Julia Pen!

Susan Oh, yes. Her name. Did you know her, Miss — er — Minister?

Julia (*suddenly aware a question has been asked*) What?

Susan Were you acquainted with the deceased?

Julia (*with an effort*) Spoken like a true reporter. I don't believe the lady was a lobby correspondent. We may have met, as we are meeting now, for a brief interview. But no more. No more.

Susan You seemed to remember her name.

Julia As I'm sure I shall remember yours.

Susan But …

Councillor Eldon-Pugh returns

Clr Eldon-Pugh We are all ready by the tea tent now. The photographer, our oldest supporter and various committee members.
Julia I look forward to seeing what you write. I read all the important press cuttings.

She returns to the chair

Clr Eldon-Pugh Our oldest supporter was a little difficult. She had the idea she was about to meet the Queen.
Susan But I never told you my name.

She shrugs and goes

The background sounds fade

Julia (*sitting*) If only …
Clr Eldon-Pugh (*to the audience*) But you are not here to listen to me …
Julia Oh, Pen …
Clr Eldon-Pugh I promised a short introduction, didn't I? So, without more ado, I give you Julia Gibbon MP.

Julia stands, moves C and acknowledges the applause while Councillor Eldon-Pugh withdraws

NB: for the rest of the play, the lines in brackets are spoken by Julia as asides

Julia Thank you. I should like to say how gratifying it is to have been invited back so soon.

Pen appears silently at the side of the stage

I have often been advised that one should first catch the attention of an audience with a laugh.

(Yes, Pen, I know you're there — still invading my thoughts.)

Observe I am telling you in advance what I propose to do. Nothing up my sleeve. That is called open government. If I can be serious for a moment though, let me tell you that I have strong opinions on open government. ...

(Go away, Pen.)

As far as I am able, I shall always try to face the public squarely.

(Must we relive that scene again and again?)

Though there will be few startling revelations on this occasion — this hardly being the occasion for startling revelations. However ...

There is the sound of soft music

Pen Jule?

Julia (*crossing to her*) I don't have long. I must be back in the House by ten.

Pen So what's new about that?

Julia Dammit, Pen, an MP has commitments. I had to break one engagement and cut another short just to get here at all.

Pen Thanks.

Julia I wasn't asking for thanks.

Pen Thanks all the same.

Julia If I only had the time ...

Pen Ah, yes.

Julia The old story. Is that what you're going to say? As long as your deadlines are met, you can please yourself how you get there. My days are plotted out in advance, minute by minute, round the clock. Time and motion? Don't make me laugh.

Pen If only I could.

Julia Must you be so bloody reasonable?

Pen One of us has to be.

Julia I just don't know how much longer we can go on like this ... Furtive exits, hoping nobody notices one slipping away; elaborate changes of route, hoping one doesn't get the same taxi-driver twice; constant glancing over your shoulder, hoping some snotty little journalist isn't on one's trail.

Pen Hold on, ducks. I'm one of your snotty little journalists.

Julia "Junior Minister in Sex Scandal."

Pen "Junior Minister in *Gay* Sex Scandal" would make a better headline.

Julia Why not "Junior Minister in Gay Sex Scandal with Suspected Subversive"?

Pen I object to "suspected". I'm a pain in the private parts to both your Houses and proud of it. I've never made any secret of my associations.

Julia All the more reason why I have to. You could dance naked down Whitehall singing "The Wearing of the Green" and not attract more than a couple of inches at the bottom of an inside page. I make one slip of the tongue and alarm bells start ringing in the world's press agencies.

Pen No need to worry about Freudian slips, my dear. You'll always be in perfect control. Never given yourself wholly to anything, have you, my love? Not that I'm blaming you. Total commitment is such a disadvantage for a politician — it rules out back-flipping when the going gets rough.

Julia Pen …

Pen I mean it takes two to quarrel. Sorry, love, but I won't. If your feelings have changed, just say so. Feelings do, and the only thing to be done with a dead love is to give it a decent burial. If you want out, you only have to ask. But no parliamentary histrionics, please. Let's have no bitter after-taste.

Julia I have responsibilities. To my constituents. To the Party …

Pen And your feelings?

Julia With an election coming up the rats are snuffling for goodies. Sex and politics! What a beanfeast!

Pen You do still have feelings?

Julia With a three thousand majority every vote counts.

Pen Counts more than what?

Julia A mere whisper could let the other side in.

Pen Counts more than us? God knows we've had little enough, but do you really want to end it?

Julia You know very well I can't. I can't. I can't!

Pen There, love.

Julia Oh, Pen, how is this going to turn out?

Pen Miserably, I suppose. Like all the best love stories. Imagine Romeo and Juliet living happily ever after. We have what we have.

Julia It won't last.

Pen Then we'll have had what we had.

Julia Always so damned reasonable. Hitting out at you is like beating an overstuffed pillow. Why don't you hit back?

Pen I reserve my temper for the right targets. Then in a showdown I don't have to pull my punches.

There is the brief sound of an angry crowd

Julia The rally this weekend …

Pen Oh, you've heard about that.

Julia We're not as ill-informed as you may suppose.

Pen Not to mention fly posters on every flat surface for miles around.

Julia What is the point of it all?

Pen Didn't you stop to read any of them?

Julia What good will it do?

Pen Stir up a little apathy, maybe. Anti-nuke, anti-job-losses, troops out … Does it matter what as long as we get up the noses of the Establishment? Remind those in high places that underdogs can at least bark.

Julia You're no underdog.

Pen So I bark on behalf of those who've forgotten how.

Julia They won't thank you.

Pen I'm not asking them to. And all the while you'll be gracious at a garden party.

Julia How did you know?

Pen Oh, we're not as ill-informed et cetera, et cetera. As a matter of fact you told me yourself. Were you hoping I might cover it? "Junior Minister reveals future thinking at fund-raising fête."

Julia Pen, love. Give that rally a miss.

Pen Oh, duckie. You know me better than that.

Julia I'm not saying join my audience. Just go for a long walk, go to a matinée, read a book, knit a blanket square for overseas aid … But stay away from that rally.

Pen Do you know something you're not telling me? Come clean, Julia.

Julia There's always a risk, and police are bound to be out in force.

Pen We're relying on them to double the headcount.

Julia For my sake, Pen.

Pen Isn't that an egocentric point of view?

Julia I don't know what I'd do without you.

Pen Nobody's indispensable.

Julia With you I can drop my defences. Say what I feel. There is nobody else.

Pen What an admission from old Ironclad herself. But definitely off the record I take it.

Julia I mean every word.

Pen Of course you do.

Julia But you don't believe me.

Pen I believe you.

Brief flash of sound: crowd and horses neighing

Julia Then for God's sake stay away from that rally.

Pen Would you cancel your junketing if I asked nicely?

Julia That's not the same.

Pen Tit for tat, ducks.

Julia There'll be no mounted police at a garden party.

Pen Mounted, eh? I must take good care not to lose my marbles.

Julia This is no joke.

Pen Who's joking? I will if you will. That's a promise.

Julia The rally won't be cancelled if you're not there. If I were to drop out now, there'd be questions leading heaven knows where. You'd not even be missed.

Pen I'd miss me.

Julia One little thing I'm asking — just one. And it's too much.

Pen I've never tried to tell you what to say or do. I might laugh at you, but I've never tried to change any part of you. I'm too fond of you as you are. If you sometimes strike me as a prejudiced, overbearing git, well — that's you. I wouldn't want you any other way. But, like I said, love — tit for tat. You must take me for what I am, too.

Julia A bloody fool.

Pen Maybe.

Julia Can't you see that every futile lunacy like this makes our position even more impossible? Can't you see that every time one of your imbecile capers hits the tabloids you put me in the firing line, too. Can't you see, or don't you want to see?

Pen Cool down, Julia. That's beginning to sound like real temper.

Julia Do you want the dirt-diggers to start shovelling?

Pen Aren't you being a wee bit one-sided — even for a pillar of the Establishment?

Julia Stop laughing, will you?

Pen One of us has to if this isn't to end in tears.

Julia You don't care, do you?

Pen I care. Maybe too much. If only I didn't.

Julia That isn't caring. It's bloody self-indulgence.

Pen Words. Only words. You're good with words. Perhaps we ought to swap jobs.

Brief burst of sound: crowd, horses and screams

Julia I've tried pleading, argument, threats, bribes and promises. I'd go down on my knees if I had the time. What else can I do to make you change your mind?

Pen Nothing, love.

Julia I have to go.

Pen So soon?

Julia I'm late already.

Pen Look both ways before you cross the road.

Julia Damn you, Pen.

She breaks away, c

Pen Love you, too, Julia.

Pen exits

The music fades

Julia resumes her speech

Julia I am talking to you now about confidence. The confidence that comes, not only from doing the right thing, but from the knowledge that one is seen to be doing the right thing. Firm government needs — demands — firm support.

Sound: street background

Susan enters

Put bluntly — to know that you are behind us. Stable government demands the backing of the governed which, in a democracy, means the electorate — in other words, of you.
(What is the morbid fascination with funerals that brings out such oddballs as forgotten relations, lovers and even such low-life as — reporters?)
Susan Oh, Miss Gibbon ...
Julia Do I know you?
Susan (*coming up to a respectful distance*) Susan Little.
Julia Susan —— ?
Susan We met at a garden party a few ——
Julia Oh, yes. The *Gazette*, wasn't it?
Susan The *Echo*.
Julia Have you been promoted to funerals?
Susan Should I have said "Minister"?
Julia Miss Gibbon will do. I should explain I'm here in a semi-private capacity. Not available for interviews.

Susan Oh?

Julia Damn! Now I suppose I'll have to elaborate to avoid the press drawing outlandish conclusions.

Susan Oh, I wouldn't ——

Julia The verdict was accidental death but, as the incident brought police action into question, my office became involved peripherally. Can you spell peripherally?

Susan I'm not taking notes, Minister.

Julia Better not let your editor know that.

Susan I haven't been sent by the paper. I took the day off.

Julia A fan of the deceased?

Susan To tell the truth, I'd never heard of her before the accident. I think it's rather sad that she had to die to make headlines.

Julia A determined reporter will do anything to make the headlines … I'd rather you didn't quote that. I'm not as unsympathetic as I may sound. The accident ought never to have happened, but it was just an unfortunate accident. That's all. The police were entirely exonerated — you'll find exonerated in the dictionary. But I really am sorry. Now, if you'll excuse me, I must look for a taxi.

Susan No official car, Minister?

Julia As I said, I'm not here officially. An absurd gesture, would you say?

Susan Beyond the call of duty. After all, until the accident, you didn't know the deceased, either, did you?

Julia I'd — heard of the deceased.

Susan Were you a fan?

Julia Say I felt an interest in the case — that is, if you must say anything. Nothing to shed tears over. But any unnecessary death, such as this, is — is … I mean…

Susan Ask not for whom the bell tolls.

Julia In a cliché — yes.

Susan Any other MPs here?

Julia This was a small private ceremony, not a state occasion.

Susan But you came.

Julia And I told you why.

Susan Of course, Minister. You told me.
Julia Big scoop! … Taxi. Hey, taxi!
Susan Could be, Minister.
Julia What did you say?
Susan It's not important, Minister.

Susan exits

Julia Taxi! Here!

The street sounds fade

Julia pulls herself together

Julia This is no time for waverers. Remember what happened to
Messrs Mistrust, Little Faith, Timorous and Facing-Both-Ways.
(Better not ask what is happening to Julia Gibbon.)
In case you don't remember your *Pilgrim's Progress*, let me
remind you that they all failed to each The Promised Land. They
didn't even believe in it. But we believe. We all know what we are
working for. But Giant Despair still lives in Doubting Castle.
(Correction—Despair can be seen any day in the bar of the House
of Commons.)

Sound: bar noises

*Dr Semple enters, glass in hand, and strolls to a pace away from
Julia*

Dr Semple Spare a minute?
Julia (*turning suddenly*) What? Oh, Doctor Semple, I presume.
Dr Semple Budgie die, then?
Julia Budgie?
Dr Semple Just a random shot. Might have been a cat or dog; but
you never struck me as a cat or dog person.
Julia I've never been a pet person of any sort.

Dr Semple Pity … Another? Gin and something? Or just gin? Or just something?

Julia Alcohol's no use for solving problems. You're left with two headaches for the price of one.

Dr Semple Speaking from experience?

Julia Brief but painful. Not to be repeated. What did you mean by pity?

Dr Semple I'm not just another MP, you know. Used to be GP.

Julia I'm not in need of a doctor.

Dr Semple Why not let a doctor give an opinion on that?

Julia Well, Doctor Semple?

Dr Semple Dark circles round the eyes usually mean something.

Julia Like not sleeping.

Dr Semple I'd sometimes prescribe a pet. Not available over the chemist's counter, but cheaper in the long run than Valium and not as addictive.

Julia I don't believe in unnecessary medication.

Dr Semple You can talk to a pet. Not that they often answer back, but that isn't important. Letting the words out can be.

Julia What words?

Dr Semple Only the patient knows till they start. "Can't stand my boss/spouse/in laws." "Why did it/didn't it happen to me?" "What if/when?"

Julia Well, time to get back to the grindstone …

Dr Semple Then they can come out in a rush — like opening a bottle. Until the cork's pulled, they're in there fermenting away. All very well for champagne, but human beings haven't got that reinforced dent at the bottom. Can't take the strain. They explode. Messy.

Julia So?

Dr Semple I'm told hamsters make agreeable pets. Don't take much looking after. You can tell your deepest, darkest secrets to a hamster and be quite sure he won't leak them to The Opposition.

Julia I share my secrets with the Under-Secretary.

Dr Semple Can you cry on an Under-Secretary's shoulder?

Julia This near the end of a parliamentary session there's no time for anybody to cry.

Dr Semple Tears can be antiseptic. Very soothing.
Julia What are you trying to get at?
Dr Semple Me?
Julia Is this probing supposed to lead anywhere?
Dr Semple Do me a favour?
Julia Ah. At least the lead-up was unorthodox.
Dr Semple I know a little restaurant …

Dr Semple takes Julia's arm and leads her to the side of the stage

The bar sounds fade

Julia and Dr Semple turn

Julia The place is full.

Sound: a small but full restaurant

Dr Semple There'll be a place in a minute. Their coq au vin is worth
  waiting for.
Julia I'm not in the habit of wasting time merely eating.
Dr Semple I can think of worse habits. Lunches of milk and
  sandwiches …
Julia Quick, satisfying and nutritionally balanced.
Dr Semple You know the saying about Nature's way of telling you
  to slow down. … That table should be free soon … If you hadn't
  agreed that I'm at least partly right, you'd never have agreed to
  come … Yes, the young lady's companion is ready to pay the bill.
Julia Oh, no!
Dr Semple Does she recognize you?
Julia I recognize her and that's enough.
Dr Semple She looks harmless.
Julia A harmless investigative journalist?
Dr Semple For the school magazine, I presume. Well, if doctors
  and policemen are getting younger, why not reporters?
Julia She has some bee in her bonnet about — never mind. But how
  did she know … ? She must have been lying in wait.

Dr Semple I think she's trying to make up her mind — should she smile or shouldn't she?

Julia If she comes over here …

Dr Semple Unless she goes out through the kitchen, she can't do anything else.

Julia We're not staying.

Dr Semple Running away? From what?

Julia Damn your amateur psychology.

Dr Semple I object to "amateur".

Julia I have nothing to say to her.

Dr Semple "Good-afternoon" in passing is usually sufficient.

Julia Do you imagine she'll let it go at that?

Dr Semple Do you suppose she can make anything of two MPs lunching together?

Julia But here!

Dr Semple You've been here before?

Julia It holds — certain memories. She knew I'd be back.

Dr Semple Put on your "meet the press" smile, Julia. It won't hurt much.

Susan comes up to them

Susan Miss Gibbon?

Julia Who else were you expecting? This is Doctor Semple.

Susan Member for Boughton.

Dr Semple The young lady's done her homework.

Susan I'm afraid I can't claim much credit. My friend recognized you. A lobby correspondent. Reporters outnumber MPs here any day. But I expect you know that.

Julia Why should I?

Susan I thought everyone knew.

Julia And what everyone doesn't know, you'll be delighted to tell them. Exclusive revelations. The name of my hairdresser, for instance? My brand of bath salts?

Susan I'm too far down the ladder yet for that.

Julia But what a leg up the right story might be.

Susan We can all dream, Miss Gibbon.

Julia Oh, some of you can do more than that, spinning your webs. Well, what particular fly were you and your collaborator hoping to catch today?

Susan We're just good friends. Believe it or not, we came here to eat.

Julia That's about as believable as Mr and Mrs Smith in a hotel register.

Dr Semple There can be a lot of truth in clichés. That's why they become clichés.

Julia Then here are some more. That horse won't run. You are on the wrong track. That game's played out. Why don't you just go back to your local rag? You're out of your depth here.

Susan You're right, Miss Gibbon …

Julia Ah!

Susan I don't know what you're on about.

Julia Coincidence, harassment, call it what you will. Which ever way I turn I find you under my feet.

Susan I'm sorry if … I mean, I don't remember. Only the garden party and the funeral.

Julia For the last time — the name Penelope Wright means nothing to me.

Dr Semple Penelope who?

Julia I wish to heaven I'd never heard it.

Susan But, Miss Gibbon …

Julia (*snapping*) Peter to you.

Dr Semple Peter?

Julia I mean — Minister. You presume too much on a very short acquaintance. In future kindly refer to me as Minister.

Susan Yes, Minister. Any time.

Susan exits

Dr Semple That table's free now.

Julia I'm not hungry.

Dr Semple Peter, eh?

Julia I was thinking of someone else. A Freudian slip.

Dr Semple Oh, very. I can't recall any Penelope Wright, but even a backsliding freethinker knows what Peter did. Perhaps COQ au vin isn't such a good idea today.

Julia My guard was down. It won't happen again. I'm in control.

Dr Semple So we all think. Now how about a glass of milk and a sandwich …

Dr Semple exits

Julia returns C

Julia I … That is …

She stumbles and hesitates for a few seconds while readjusting to her surroundings

I'm sorry — an unfortunate twinge of memory. I thought I recognized … (*She peers into the audience*) Ah, yes. So it is. The *Echo*. … I was suddenly reminded of an occasion when a brash young reporter — *another*, different, brash young reporter: yes, indeed, young lady, there have been others — a young reporter asked if there had been anything in my career that I might have regretted. I replied that my only regret lay in having nothing to regret.

Pen enters and stands silently at the side of the stage

Gradually the asides become direct addresses to Pen

Julia So tell your editor to stick that on his spike and shred it.
(Yes, Pen, I know you're still there.)
Recently there have been rumours about the private lives of persons in the public eye spread by certain tabloids.
(You're dead, Pen. This is taking an unfair advantage.)

I can categorically state that I, personally, have nothing to hide. I only hope certain gutter journalists can say as much. (What do you expect from me — tears?) I repeat — there has been nothing in my past that I regret. Does that satisfy you aspiring young muckrakers? Sorry, but you won't be getting any more. For persons in my position a public display of private grief is a luxury beyond our means. (*With a little forced laugh*) We remember what happened to Lord Lundy, who was too easily moved to tears — "Be off, and govern New South Wales". (What's past is past. Crying won't bring it back.) But I digress. I was talking about confidence … I … (For God's sake, Pen, you're dead and gone. You don't exist any longer. For me now you never existed. You're out of my life: stay out of my mind.)

Pen withdraws

I never knew her, you understand. She was never part of my life. I have no tears to shed for her. … Pen? … Gone? … Really gone? … Gone! … Confidence. Yes. As I was saying … What do you all expect of me. Business as usual? I tried. God knows, I tried. But every creature has a right to grieve. Why not me? "A widow bird sat mourning for her mate upon a wintry bough." Does a politician count for less than the birds of air or the beasts of the field? She's gone. Really gone. Leaving nothing but a black hole.

Councillor Eldon-Pugh appears at the side of the stage

Pen? No, you're not Pen. There's a gaping black hole where she used to be. "She is dead and gone, lady. She is dead and gone … They say she made a good end." Ophelia, you know — but she was not accountable for her actions at the time.

Clr Eldon-Pugh Miss Gibbon …

Julia Not to panic, Councillor Eldon-Pugh. I am in control. One tear drop would breach the dam, you see. After that, the deluge.

She brushes her cheek with the back of her hand, then looks at it

  One drop. Too many …

She covers her face with her hands

Councillor Eldon-Pugh hurries over to her

Clr Eldon-Pugh Miss Gibbon.

Julia is now shaken by a paroxysm of grief

  Please, Miss Gibbon …

Julia looks up, but apparently unaware of her surroundings

Julia Goodbye, sweet Pen. Was alive and is dead: there's no more
  to be said. Goodbye, sweet lady. Goodbye. Goodbye.
Clr Eldon-Pugh Is there a doctor in the house?
Julia (*momentarily pulling herself together*) No need for that. I'm
  in command of myself. I've always been in perfect command. No
  tears, by request. Hear that, Pen – wherever you are. No tears.
  Permission to cry, sir. Permission denied. I am … I am — in
  control.

*She breaks down completely, sinking to her knees as the tears flow
uncontrollably*

Councillor Eldon-Pugh flaps helplessly

Clr Eldon-Pugh Help, for goodness sake. Someone … Anyone!
  Please help! … So embarrassing. Why can't people show decent
  restraint?

CURTAIN

FURNITURE AND PROPERTY LIST

On stage: Chair

Off stage: Glass (**Dr Semple**)

LIGHTING PLOT

To open: Full stage lighting

No cues

EFFECTS PLOT